# Cricket

# Cricket

**BOB FARMER**

*Geschenk für den offenen Bücherschrank*

**Hamlyn**

London · New York · Sydney · Toronto

# Contents

Foreword 7

Chapter One
Introduction 8

Chapter Two
Batting 9

Chapter Three
Bowling 25

Chapter Four
Fielding 38

Chapter Five
Wicketkeeping 43

Chapter Six
Captaincy 50

Chapter Seven
The Game's Structure 53

*Glossary* 59

*Acknowledgments* 60

*Index* 61

Published by
The Hamlyn Publishing Group Limited
London · New York · Sydney · Toronto
Astronaut House, Feltham, Middlesex, England

© Copyright The Hamlyn Publishing Group Limited 1984
Originally published as *How to play Cricket*

All rights reserved. No part of this publication may be reproduced, stored in a retrieval system, or transmitted, in any form or by any means, electronic, mechanical, photocopying, recording or otherwise without the permission of The Hamlyn Publishing Group Limited

ISBN 0 600 34785 0

Printed in Italy

# Foreword

Cricket in the last ten years has enjoyed such an upsurge of enthusiasm that today's younger generation are flocking to a game which appeared to be dying on its feet through lack of interest in the 1960s.

The revolution was brought about by the introduction of limited-overs cricket in which each side bats for a set number of overs and matches are completed in a day, often in the most exciting circumstances.

The main criticism of cricket had been the slow tempo that made the game both tedious and too often bedevilled by drawn matches. Limited-overs cricket ensured a result.

While recognising and applauding 'instant' cricket, I must stress that this book is aimed at instructing the student in the technically correct way to play cricket – and the point is stressed because the limited-overs game does occasionally depart from the textbook.

For although cricket has become a two-tiered game – the genuine article and the 'instant' variety – basic instruction must be drawn from the way the game has been played for 100 years. This book also assumes that the reader has a smattering of knowledge of how cricket is played, but a booklet of the complete rules is available on application to Lord's Cricket Ground, St John's Wood, London NW8.

# Chapter One
# Introduction

Cricket, like the Royal Family, is one of those English institutions without which, we are fondly told, the country would collapse. Certainly the grand old game has been played literally for centuries. There is, after all, mention of Edward the First's son playing Creag in 1272 and an existing manuscript from 1598 stating that the Surrey coroner was 'playing at crickett'.

Cricket is, indeed, a most complex game, but it is basically a battle of wits between batting and bowling. Most players become proficient in one or other of these skills; only exceptional players shine at both and become known as 'allrounders'. This book sets out to explain how to attempt to excel in either capacity, but also points out the various other aspects of the game . . . fielding, wicketkeeping and captaincy as well as outlining the main competitions. Left-handed players should remember to reverse all the specific instructions given in the text and everyone should become familiar with the field placings shown in the diagram.

Whatever your level of ability, remember that there is, after all, a place for everybody in cricket. It does not demand any specific level of physical or of muscular ability, yet at the same time it is probably the most individualistic team game in existence.

Its popularity today is unsurpassed with even a World Cup competition every four years which attracts the most improbable of countries. For cricket is, without doubt, habit-forming. Once 'hooked' on the game there is no escape. Now read on and polish up your performance – even if you do not become a great player, you will be eternally grateful for having become addicted to the game of cricket.

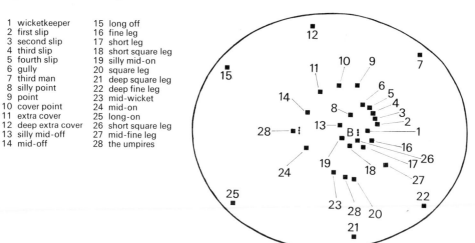

**Diagram 1:** The most common field placings for a right-handed batsman:

1 wicketkeeper
2 first slip
3 second slip
4 third slip
5 fourth slip
6 gully
7 third man
8 silly point
9 point
10 cover point
11 extra cover
12 deep extra cover
13 silly mid-off
14 mid-off
15 long off
16 fine leg
17 short leg
18 short square leg
19 silly mid-on
20 square leg
21 deep square leg
22 deep fine leg
23 mid-wicket
24 mid-on
25 long-on
26 short square leg
27 mid-fine leg
28 the umpires

# Chapter Two
# Batting

A bad workman will always blame the tools of his trade for a poor performance, but this excuse cannot be put forward for a bad batsman provided a few simple principles are observed in the choice and care of his equipment. The basics for a batsman are an ideally weighted bat of the correct size plus the protective pads and gloves.

The bat should never be too heavy – always find weight and length that matches your own strength and weight.

Ideally a man of average height – 5 feet 10 inches – will have a bat 2 feet 11 inches long and about 2·4 pounds heavy. A schoolboy of between 5 feet 3 inches and 5 feet 5 inches will bat with one 2 feet 9 inches long and weighing about 2·2 pounds.

Having bought your bat, cosset it. Use linseed oil on the face about halfway down, where the ball is most often going to be struck. When the surface becomes so hard that it does not soak in the oil, use a scraper to remove the film off the surface.

Pads are purely a question of comfort, but don't forget to have them well whitened before a match. Spectators, after all, still expect to see cricketers smartly turned out. In the commercial modern cricket world, many styles of batting gloves have come on the market. Again, however, it is simply a case of personal preference.

On the subject of modern cricket, one item of protection has to be mentioned in deference to its disciples – the crash helmet! Perish the possibility that this may become a commonplace in schoolboy cricket, but if a senior player feels sufficiently unnerved by the speed of a fast bowler then there is nothing in the rules to

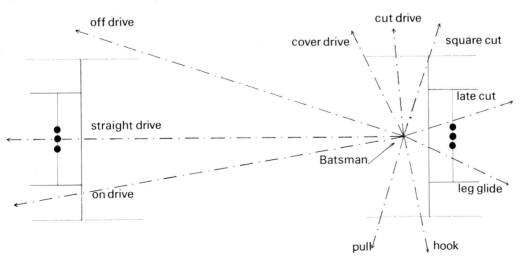

Diagram 2: The batsman's strokes.

prevent him placing one on his head. But avoid the indignity if you can.

The correct way to grip your bat is to have both hands close together and reasonably high on the handle. The reason is that if the bat is held lower down the handle, your leverage, reach and swing are reduced, too. The left hand is above the right (for a left-handed batsman the instructions are reversed) with the back of the left hand facing towards the bowler with both thumbs around the handle. Use all the fingers of the left hand to grip the bat because this hand has to control the movement of the bat.

After the grip comes the stance and here comfort is the key. Either foot should be able to move freely, so the weight should be distributed evenly between both feet. It does not matter whether the feet are together or a little apart. Shoulders should be pointed down the pitch towards the bowler (cricket is very much a 'side on' game) otherwise a two-eyed stance will occur with the left shoulder, instead of pointing at the bowler, leaving an open and ungainly stance and also making the offside shot that much more difficult to execute.

To see the ball correctly and as soon as it leaves the hand of the bowler, the eyes must be at the same distance from the ball so that the head faces directly down the wicket. This is to get a clear indication of where the ball is likely to pitch and maximum time to decide on the shot to be played.

Timing of the shot depends on flexible wrists. They should

Viv Richards (Somerset and the West Indies) demonstrates a good orthodox stance. Sideways-on to the bowler and evenly balanced on both feet, the batsman should always be watching the bowler with his eyes perfectly level to get the best perspective on the delivery.

never be kept stiff for this would reduce the strength of the shot.

Use of the wrists in making a stroke is as follows: the bat is lifted back at first by bending the wrists and arms and as the ball is played on the downward movement the arms move first and the wrists come into action just before the ball is hit.

Wrists can also correct errors of timing in the arm movement. If the arms have brought the bat down too soon, a slow movement of the wrists will delay the bat in the last stage before the ball arrives. Likewise, if the arms bring the bat down too late, very speedy movement of the wrists can get the bat there in time. In fact, skilful use of the wrists in the vital instant before impact shows the ability of a batsman.

## Concentration

While batting might seem a simple exercise batsmen at all levels lose their wicket by relaxing on seeing a bad ball, lifting their heads and failing to follow intently the flight of the ball.

Always remember to watch the flight of the delivery. From the moment that the bowler starts to run in, the batsman must watch the ball. Even if he is finding it hard to score runs, he will be very hard to dismiss if he has a sound concentration.

With concentration comes commitment to the decision on how to play the ball. As it approaches, the ball can do many devious things, either through the air or off the pitch. Thus a batsman should not commit himself until he has learnt all he can about the delivery.

Time to make a stroke depends on the speed of footwork. Many batsmen commit themselves too early and can be caught napping by a late deviation in the delivery.

A disciplined batsman is one who will always wait as long as he can before committing himself to the stroke.

It is a useful tip to have someone serve the ball from halfway down the pitch in practice. It gives the batsman no time to move too early and can only improve his technique.

## Forward Stroke

The forward stroke is played to deal with a delivery that can be reached before or just after it has pitched.

All the weight is put on the right foot, leaving the left foot free to move forward. The left hand controls the movement of the bat which should be held with a low backlift. Then, just as the bat starts coming down, the left foot should be advanced close to the pitch of the ball with the body's weight transferred.

At the point of contact, the left leg is bent at the knee while the right foot just touches the ground with the toe fractionally inside the batting crease to avoid the possibility of a sharp stumping should the ball be missed. The head should be well forward with the eyes level and directly in line with the bat handle and the ball is met directly beneath the eyes.

*Above:* The forward defensive stroke. The bat is brought down on line with the delivery while the left foot moves forward towards the pitch of the ball. When the ball is struck the batsman should be directly above the ball and looking down on it over the top of the handle.

Make sure to get right up to the pitch and have the left foot alongside the ball. Failure to do so and to play the ball right in front of the left foot will often result in popping up a catch to the bowler as he follows through after delivering the ball.

### Back Stroke

While the forward stroke is both a model method of defence and a handsome scoring stroke, the back stroke can be just as beneficial.

The back stroke is played for deliveries that are not pitched up enough to play forward – or for an exceptionally overpitched full toss. The awkwardly-pitched ball automatically must force the batsman back in defence of his wicket. The back stroke becomes an effective scoring shot when the bowler pitches too short, leaving plenty of time to lean back, watch the ball coming onto the bat and punch it away for what should prove a prolific scoring shot.

Footwork and body balance are just as important as for the forward stroke, except that the footwork is reversed. The weight must be transferred to the left foot as the right leg is moved back with bat uplifted. The head, as ever, should be on line with the ball with eyes level and left shoulder and elbow high, the left hand controlling the bat with the right hand grip relaxed.

The ball is met immediately below the eyes with the weight of the body on the back foot. The right foot should be well back towards the stumps, but parallel to the crease.

## The Drive

There is no more satisfying shot in cricket – for batsman and spectator alike – than the perfectly executed drive. The shot

*Left:* The cover drive. Here the batsman has moved down the wicket and hit the ball hard and high. In the follow-through the head and the bat remain on line with the ball after the stroke has been made.

*Below opposite:* The back defensive stroke. The right foot moves back to and parallel with the crease creating a more open stance. The ball is struck with the full face of the bat and at impact the hands are slightly in front of the ball to keep it low.

consists of an almost complete swing of the bat to hit the ball immediately after it has pitched.

There are two methods of driving. If the ball is pitched well up, then the left foot advances while the right foot remains rooted in the crease. But if the ball is pitched shorter, the batsman can advance down the wicket to meet the ball on the half-volley.

Commitment, commented on earlier, plays an important part in the playing of the shot. No thoughts of being stumped should enter the batsman's mind otherwise any hesitation will probably mean a failure to get to the pitch of the ball.

With the first method of driving – with the right foot remaining grounded – there are some differences from the ordinary forward stroke. The bat is raised with a much higher backlift, both hands should grip the handle tightly and a turn of the wrists makes the blade face the position of point fielder when the bat is at the top of its lift. The movement forward of the left foot is shorter, the body is fairly upright and the left leg unbent. The bat must travel in the direction that the ball will take and stay on this course after it has actually been hit for the full follow-through to give maximum force. The weight of the body should continue to travel in the direction of the shot with the left shoulder and hip remaining firm (not, in other words, swinging round as in a golfer's swing) with the right shoulder released so that when the stroke has been completed the batsman's chest should be in line with the bowler.

The on drive. Again the batsman has advanced down the wicket and steered the ball towards mid-on.

*Above and above left:* The end of an off drive by Barry Richards. Both the front foot and the bat aim directly at point and the bat continues on line in a high follow-through after striking the ball.

A bouncer from Bob Willis is hooked for four runs.

The cut. As the delivery begins, the batsman pivots back to the right and transfers his weight to the back foot. The ball is then hit down with the wrists flexible and the arms perfectly straight and in line with the bat to make one long lever.

Moving out to drive means taking a long stride down the pitch with the left foot while the right foot glides up behind the left heel so that the feet are crossed. The weight is transferred to the right foot from where the normal drive is played. If, however, the batsman realises he is unable to make the ball into a half-volley, the intended drive must be changed to the orthodox forward stroke. Failure to do so would result in spooning the ball into the air for a probable catch.

**The Cut**

This shot comes into that category of strokes known as 'cross-batted' and is played with the right foot moving across the wicket, the ball normally being played behind the point fielder. Square cuts will probably travel down in the direction of the third man position and late cuts along the ground past second slip. It is a shot that requires some finesse and timing and should not really be attempted before the batsman has been in for some time, has judged the pace of the wicket and is seeing the ball well. The most effective balls for cutting are those of medium pace, delivered short and veering outside off stump. Lift the bat well up, as with the drive, moving the right foot back towards the wicket and facing offside just behind the point position. Wait until the ball is almost through then bring the arms abruptly down with the intention of hitting well up on the bat. Thus, with the weight on the right foot and the bat thrown hard at the ball in the direction it is taking, you can put real power into the shot. Arms should be straight and wrists rolling.

However, it is dangerous to try the shot at a slow bowler. With the ball coming through slowly, your timing can be too early and the end result is an edged catch to the slips. Even if the shot is executed correctly against the slow bowler, the lack of pace in the delivery means that however hard you play the shot, the ball will not travel with much force into the field and, at best, you will only score a single for your trouble.

**The Hook**
Again a cross-batted stroke but differing from the cut in that it is designed to hit the ball to the legside. Also, it is probably the most belligerent shot in the book and, in consequence, one of the most risky. At its most effective, the one that will bring you most sixes . . . or caught on the boundary dismissals!

The hook is employed against the short-pitched ball coming at some speed – in other words the infamous 'bouncer' – and rising to some height. With not much time to decide, the choice is to duck or go for the hook. And speedy footwork is of the essence.

The right foot goes all the way back and to the off stump so that it is outside the line of flight, whereas head and shoulders are in line and facing the bowler. Lift the bat outwards in the direction of third man and then sweep across the chest.

If the batsman has been at the crease for some time and is supremely confident then he will be prepared to keep his bat going in an arc up towards his left shoulder and sky the ball up over the boundary for six. Technically, however, he should be bringing the bat downwards as he sweeps it across his chest so that the ball will be played downwards to deny the fielders any chance of a catch. That, of course, is not so spectacular and, at best, will bring only a boundary four.

The hook. As the ball is bowled the batsman moves across the off stump to gain more time and space and sweeps across his chest. Here Philip Slocombe (Somerset) has kept the ball low by turning his wrists as he plays the shot so that the bat ends facing downwards.

But the ambitious batsman would do well to realise that the short-pitched ball or 'bouncer' is something of a 'sucker' ball that is used to tempt aggressive batsmen with a weakness for hooking to sky a catch into the arc between square and long leg. This happens at the highest level of cricket with Test Match bowlers 'buying' wickets by tempting top stars. An example occurred in the 1978 Gillette Cup final when the West Indian Viv Richards, undoubtedly the greatest batsman in the world today, fell for the short-pitched ball and hooked straight into square leg's hands. It was a spectacular shot, but it cost his county the Cup. Therein the danger of this most thrilling of shots.

## The Pull Shot

It is related to the hook, but is a much safer shot to play. It is

The pull shot. Safer than the hook, but with basically the same action. The bat is raised into a high backlift and swung forcefully down to make contact with the ball at full stretch.

used to attack the slow bowler – particularly in pulling against a leg break – or to take advantage of a wicket with no life in it.

As with the hook, the right foot goes back and outside the line of flight which brings the head and shoulders into line with the ball. The bat is raised high and comes down at the ball with the body facing somewhat more to the offside than with the hook. The stroke is played well in front of the body and, as the bat swings from off to leg, the weight is transferred onto the left foot. The effect is a fairly hard-hit shot somewhere in the square leg to midwicket area.

## Scoring to Leg

The legside should be where the vast majority of runs are scored in cricket and, unless he is a leg break specialist, no bowler willingly aims down legside. Yet batsmen often miss out on legside scoring since a ball pitched thereabouts often seems the signal for a batsman to lose concentration, stop watching the ball intently and swing or wave wildly at it.

For most balls on leg, the action to take is a modification of the forward or back stroke. If the ball is well pitched up, a forward stroke is played with the left leg kept out of the way. This enables the bat to swing across and hit the ball in front of square leg with the right foot pivoting round. With shorter balls on or just outside leg, play the backstroke. And for really wide balls, use a crossbat method.

The leg flick. Viv Richards begins his run after gliding the ball towards square leg.

The leg push. Barry Richards shows how the bat must be kept vertical when the ball is struck. If played correctly, this stroke can harvest a useful number of singles.

Run scoring can be profitable from the leg push. The shot is made from the shorter ball with the batsman moving his feet for the backstroke with the right foot facing down the wicket and the left shoulder turned towards mid-wicket. The ball can be pushed or guided into gaps on the legside. For the faster short ball, the shot becomes a flick or glide fine down the legside.

The crossbat shot is correctly known as the sweep. It is a natural swing across the body with the right hand doing all the controlling of the bat. The left leg should be well across, both elbows should be bent so that the ball is hit with the bat's full force and aimed in front of square leg. As in the case of the hook, keep the bat swinging in a downward movement or otherwise the ball will lob up into a catch.

The sweep can look somewhat unsightly if badly executed and is often confused with the old-fashioned cowshot you can see on any village green. Whereas the correct sweep is played to a ball pitching outside leg stump, the cowshot comes from trying to swing round to leg from a ball that is on line with middle or off stump. It is technically atrocious and much beloved of tailend batsmen with few pretensions to the finer points of batting . . . often effective in a hectic pursuit of runs, but to be avoided otherwise at all costs.

The sweep. The left leg is bent to bring the batsman low enough to hit the ball with an almost horizontal bat. At contact its face should be slightly closed to keep the ball low.

## Danger Deliveries

While a bold batsman is always good to watch, he will never improve his ability unless he is able to pick out the balls that must be treated with respect.

A good length ball is one which, after bouncing, can only be struck by the upper part of the bat. This means that full meaty drive cannot be played and makes scoring very difficult when the ball is on line with the stumps or passing just outside off stump. It is as well, in fact, to leave alone the ball passing just outside the stumps otherwise there is the danger of getting a touch with the edge and offering a catch to wicketkeeper or slips. If on line, play a straight bat.

An even more effective ball for blunting a batsman's potential is the one pitched up to land just about on the batting crease. This is known as the 'yorker', which is intended to squeeze under the bottom of the bat. The batsman must drop his wrists fast to dig the ball out with the base of the bat.

## Fast Bowling

No batsman, to be truthful, really relishes flat-out fast bowling for the very human reason that he has a sneaking fear of being hit and hurt. But most fast bowlers, unless they bowl short-pitched, hittable balls or the dangerous yorker, will aim not so much at the stumps as to induce the batsman to snick a catch behind. In the early stages of an innings when the batsman is still judging the pace of the pitch it is wise for him to leave well alone and only play forward with a firm grip to those balls on line.

Playing and missing, however, is inevitable when the bowler delivers a ball that might or might not just clip the off stump and so forces a shot from the batsman. But do not despair that the fast bowler must always hold the whip hand. For one thing, the batsman does not need to hit over-hard to be assured of runs since the ball already has pace off the pitch.

And fast bowlers really can be caned if you take these tips: any short ball about a foot outside off stump can be cut for four; every ball pitched down leg can be glided to fine leg for a single or four; every half-volley can be driven back straight and will probably beat the field for sheer speed. Remember, too, that although the wicketkeeper will be waiting for a snicked catch, he has to stand so far back that the batsman can move forward to the delivery knowing there is no danger of being stumped.

The fast bowler is most dangerous in the early stages of a batsman's arrival at the crease. By being watchful and waiting for the inevitable odd bad ball, the batsman can gradually win the battle of wits.

**Slow Bowling**

The state of the wicket is the crucial factor in the playing of slow bowling.

If the wicket is hard then there should be few problems since the ball will spin or turn not much more than an inch or so in a yard. It does, however, come off the pitch at a fairly lively speed so the good-length delivery should always be played on the forward stroke, making it into a half-volley. To go back to such a ball leads to the very real danger of being trapped leg before wicket or bowled.

If the wicket is soft and slow, the spinner becomes more dangerous although the ball will, in these conditions, come off the pitch that much more slowly. Therefore, play back where possible and watch the ball come slowly onto the bat.

If the wicket has a worn patch or is 'sweating' as it dries out after recent rain, the batsman really needs to use his wits to stay out of trouble for now the ball will turn and lift sharply. But by watching the slow bowler's hand as he delivers, the batsman can discover what sort of spin he is going to have to smother.

If the ball comes from the front of the hand it will be a leg break from a right-armer. From the back of the hand, the spin will be reversed. Move out to kill the spin. When forced to play back, try to get your pads right behind your bat.

Footwork is all important in moving out to smother the ball or in turning the delivery into a full pitch. Every time you advance to

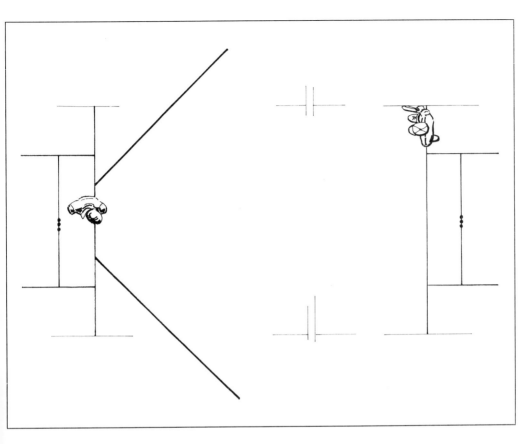

**Diagram 3**: Calling and running. The striking batsman decides if runs are possible only for balls travelling in his line of vision.

make the ball into a full pitch, you should be able to drive effectively. And when the ball is pitched too short, you can drive, square cut or pull.

**Calling and Running**

The most irritating of all dismissals for a batsman is to be run out. He may have played the perfect shot, but have been run out because of lack of judgment of the chance of making his run. Of course, the advent of limited-overs cricket and the need to take risks in a chase for runs increases this method of 'mortality' among batsmen, but in an orthodox innings it is an error that can be erased by the simple expedient of learning the correct art of calling and running.

The object of calling is for the batsman in the best position to judge to inform his partner as soon as possible whether or not a run is possible. He does this with the command 'Yes' or 'Come One'; 'Wait' means that the caller wants to make certain before committing himself and his partner to a run; 'No' is self-explanatory. The call should be crisp and clear at all times.

The question of who makes the call depends on where the ball is hit. If the striking batsman plays a shot in front of the wicket then he has a full field of vision and takes the decision. If the ball is played behind the wicket then the batsman at the non-striker's end takes responsibility.

The decision on running is determined by several factors among which are: the speed and positioning of the ball – a slow-moving ball wide of a fielder can produce a run while a harder-hit shot may not; the angle at which the ball approaches the fielder; the speed with which the striking batsman can set out on a run – he may, after all, have overbalanced in making his stroke; any knowledge acquired of a particular fielder's prowess, or lack of it.

In being ready to run, the non-striker should leave his crease as the ball is bowled and be on his toes poised to run or return to his own crease.

Where a straightforward single is there to be taken, the batsmen do not need to set out like sprinters, which would be a sheer waste of energy. But when there is the chance of converting a single into a two or more, then the first run should be made at top speed.

Finally, a batsman should not forget that his bat adds to the distance he can travel in the quickest time possible. He does not need to have his feet in the crease so long as he extends his bat to the full length of his arm and slides it over the crease. So, when running, do not grip the bat halfway down the handle and at hip-height but run with it held straight in front of you.

If your bat is grounded in the batting crease you cannot be run out so always hold the bat high on the handle and carry it well in front of you.

# Chapter Three
# Bowling

Cricket, when it comes down to the basics, really amounts to a battle of wits between batsman and bowler.

It is the bowler's job to dismiss the batsman either by having him bowled, leg before wicket, caught, stumped or, on the very rare occasion, causing him to play back so abruptly that he hits his own wicket with his bat or some part of his body. The batsman, on the other hand, has two functions: first, to avoid being dismissed; second, to score runs.

It is the bowler who holds the initiative since he determines the type of delivery – fast, medium pace or slow – and he also holds the key to whether the ball be difficult or easy to play.

The difficult delivery is one that should make the batsman think that if he misses it, it will hit his wicket. This is known as good line. The ball should also be pitched so that it arrives at an awkward angle to the bat, thereby possibly causing an unintended shot. This is known as good length. Line and length are the absolute essentials for any successful bowler.

The easy ball to play comes into three categories. First, there is the full toss, when the ball is so over-flighted that the batsman can hit before it pitches. Then there is the half-volley which can be hit with full force immediately after pitching. Finally, there is the long hop – a ball pitched very short (say halfway down the wicket) – which gives the batsman ample time to see it onto his bat and crack it away to just about any position he chooses. All these types of delivery will invariably be hit for four.

In discussing good bowling, it is worthwhile to point out that although the big-scoring batsman may seem to enjoy a more glamorous role in the game, there is really just as much to admire in the master bowler demonstrating his art, be he fast, medium or slow in his style.

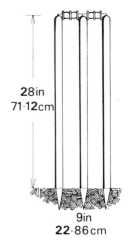

**Diagram 4:** Measurements of a cricket wicket (not to scale).

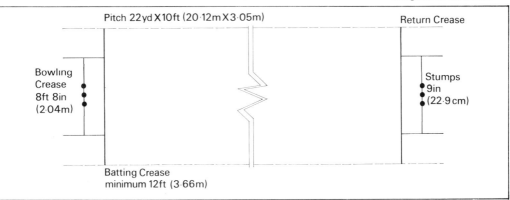

**Diagram 5:** The wicket.

A front view of fast bowler Mike Hendrick (Derbyshire and England). The ball is released at the maximum possible height before the bowler swings into a perfectly-balanced follow-through.

## Run-up and Delivery

The purpose of the run-up is to bring the bowler smoothly to the wicket with the correct speed for his style of delivery. It takes much practice to find the right length of run-up and the bowler must go through the motion time and again until it has become automatic. The main thing is to make sure that the paces are smooth and even since any shuffle halfway to the wicket means that the previous part of the run-up is a waste of time and energy. For fast and medium-pace bowlers, the run must work up pace and not be checked just before the delivery stride. Any inclination to do that and the bowler might just as well not have bothered running at all.

A side view of John Lever (Essex and England), a left-handed fast bowler.

On arrival at the wicket, the following action should occur (again we are thinking in terms of the right-hander so reverse the procedure if you are left-handed):

The right leg has arrived just behind the crease with the foot facing almost square to the legside, with left shoulder facing the batsman. The left leg advances on the vital step. As it leaves the ground it is facing the mid-on position, but as the body swing starts it pivots before landing pointing at square leg.

The body swing is generated by the run-up and work of the left arm which is raised almost vertically with the bowler looking down the wicket over the top of the left arm.

As the left foot comes to the ground, the left arm is cut away to

develop the swing of the body. The left foot comes down hard, with the left leg straight as the right shoulder swings forward in delivery. Meanwhile the right foot has left the ground and is coming through on its next step, the first stride of the follow-through.

The ball should, of course, be delivered from maximum height which means that the distance between left foot and right hand should be as much as possible at the point of delivery.

**Length and Line**

A useful way of estimating a good length ball is to pitch between six and seven yards from the batsman's wicket if bowling fast; five yards if at medium pace; four yards if slow. These distances represent the 'no man's land' between the forward and back strokes.

An easy, rhythmic delivery and persistent practice will bring control of length. The ball should be released from the highest point the hand can reach. The delivery will therefore be smooth and control of length the greater.

As for line, it is important to vary direction. Keep the batsman guessing by sending down some balls straight, some just outside off stump and, occasionally, on or just wide of leg stump.

A useful form of practice is to place a piece of paper on the target area and see how many times you can hit it in every six balls.

**Pace Variation**

After the run-up, the delivery, length and line, it is invaluable to learn how to vary the pace of your delivery whatever type of bowler you happen to be. The idea is to deceive the batsman by not changing your run-up and style of delivery in any apparent way.

The effect, when executed, can be to trap a batsman who has become accustomed to the bowler's arc of flight into playing too early or too late.

The art lies in the extent to which the wrist is used in the final

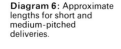

**Diagram 6**: Approximate lengths for short and medium-pitched deliveries.

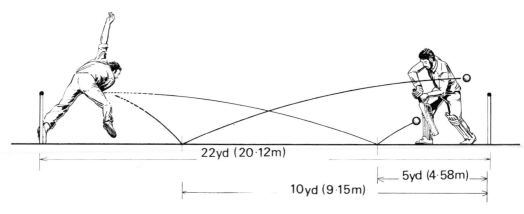

The perfect follow-through. John Snow's right foot is pointing directly at the batsman, his right hand has swung past his left thigh and his left arm has swung completely upright too.

moment of delivery. What is needed is a slight change of pace with no change of action. If the bowler flicks his wrist to full capacity the ball will come through that bit faster. If he does not use his wrist at all, then it will be that much slower. For the batsman it remains completely disguised if correctly operated.

## Fast Bowling

However strong a batting side may be, success in cricket invariably depends on top-flight fast bowling. If we just concern ourselves with the post-war era of Test cricket the decisive match-winners have been pace stars 'hunting' as a pair. England had Trueman and Statham; Australia were at their peak with Lindwall and Miller and latterly Lillee and Thomson; the West Indies once had Hall and Griffiths and, much more recently, a veritable battery of pace in players like Roberts, Holding and Daniel.

But it is an exacting job and that is why the fast bowler will operate in fairly short, sharp bursts of a few overs at a time. He can also help to avoid tiring himself out too quickly by perfecting an easy, rhythmic run-up. He has to land his right foot as far forward as the rules allow without being 'no balled' for overstepping. The run-up, too, is far from finished after the delivery of the ball. He must have a follow-through of a few paces to guard against any checking of his pace.

One point about the follow-through: the bowler should veer

Fast bowler David Gurr in action.

away from the wicket or otherwise his boots are likely to damage the area just in front of the batting crease. Umpires frequently have to warn fast bowlers about this and they have the power to remove them from the attack for the rest of an innings if they persist.

The most spectacular method of dismissal is by beating and bowling the batsman by sheer pace, perhaps with a yorker (the ball that squeezes under the bat as described earlier) or an inswinger that comes back from the off stump. But more often than not, a fast bowler's delivery will bounce over the stumps and a large proportion of his wickets will come from catches behind them.

The ball that produces these snicks and edges is invariably an

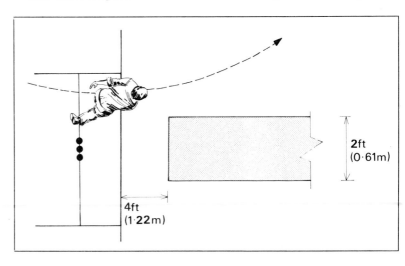

**Diagram 7**: To avoid damage to the pitch, the bowler must veer away from the shaded area.

outswinger (a ball that pitches on or just outside off stump) which the batsman is obliged to play. Ideally the late swing then finds the edge of the bat.

## The Bouncer

If the hook shot is arguably the most exciting shot in the batsman's repertoire, then the ball which induces it – the bouncer – must be the most spectacular ball from the fast bowler's point of view.

It is achieved by pitching deliberately short of a length and probably on line with leg stump and has two purposes: either to soften up a batsman by forcing him to duck hurriedly and, who knows, show signs of losing his nerve; or to tempt the bold batsman into going for the hook shot and holing out with a skied catch.

The first intention may sound somewhat unsporting and intimidatory and the recurring public rows over danger to batsmen and the crash helmets controversy have made the bouncer all but a dirty word. However, it is a legitimate enough weapon with the very important proviso that the delivery should not be overdone. A ration of two per over is the absolute maximum, but the bouncer should be used very sparingly and certainly not against a non-recognised, tailend batsman ill-equipped to defend himself.

One step further from bouncers are beamers. These are balls that fly out of the hand at a full toss and head-high. Usually they occur because the bowler loses control of the grip of the ball as he delivers. But they have been known because the bowler lost control of his temper. Never knowingly bowl them!

Two views of spinner Derek Underwood. Compare his finish position with that of Mick Hendrick on page 27.

## The Medium-Pacer

While the fast bowler only operates in short, sharp spells and the spin bowler may only expect to be employed for long spells if the state of the wicket suits him, the bowler who must bear the brunt of the work is the medium-pacer.

By definition, his is the least exacting technique and he will therefore bowl far more overs in a season on all types of wickets than the others. And since a straightforward medium-paced delivery should pose no exceptional problems for the batsman, he has to conjure up some cunning to get his wickets.

He must, in any case, acquire complete control of length, direction and variety of pace. He could, of course, just stick to a nagging line and length and hope to exasperate a batsman so much that the batsman has a wild swing and loses his wicket. But he has more subtle methods to employ.

He can bowl a few balls that pitch on off stump and move away, followed by one that breaks to leg stump or goes on with the arm, i.e. straight. By such variation, he has the batsman constantly unprepared over what to expect next. The bowler therefore needs to be able to employ swerve and spin as well as maintaining length and direction.

He also has to 'think' his opponents out by relying on patience and the knack of knowing when to pop in the unexpected delivery. He should therefore concentrate on one particular type of delivery for most of each over and then put in the unexpected ball. His 'stock' ball is usually the off break of good length and medium pace. It is the odd ball that varies which will get the wickets.

## Swerve
Making the ball swerve and change direction in flight is most common when the new ball is in use. It is the shiny, polished surface which produces the swerve either from the off or legside, known respectively as inswing or outswing.

The off swerve comes with the arm up over the head and away from the body on the downward movement. A slightly round arm swing produces outswing from the legside.

Making the ball swerve, however, is a lucky knack that comes more easily to the action of some bowlers than others. England's young allrounder Ian Botham is one such bowler, but even he needs the weather conditions to complement his swerve. In heavy, overcast and sultry weather the swerve can be amazingly pronounced – on a clear day there may be no movement at all.

## Spin Bowling
Fast bowlers may be the front line of a fielding team's attack, medium-pacers may have most of the work to do on an average day, but the spin bowler is the real stylist. While the fast bowler relies on sheer speed and swerve, the spinner is the subtle tactician involved in a battle of wits with the batsman.

Spin bowling is basically about producing a change of direction

The basic grip for seam bowling. The thumb is on the seam and the first and second fingers are on either side of it holding it very lightly.

after the ball has pitched. It may change direction from the offside (off break), legside (leg break) or speed straight through off the pitch (top spin).

The spinner does not need the ball to have its early shine still, although it should be dry. A wet ball will make length and direction difficult.

Ideal conditions are when a wicket which has been wet and soft is drying out under the sun. There is sponginess under a thin surface hardness. The sponginess helps the spin to bite, the surface hardness gives speed off the pitch. In these sort of conditions a masterly spinner can create utter chaos, Kent's former England player Derek Underwood being nicknamed 'Deadly' in such situations.

Very dry, hard wickets are of no help to the spinner, while soft, damp wickets slow the ball down and although there is still spin, the batsman has plenty of time to watch the ball onto his bat.

### Off Breaks and Leg Breaks

Fingers play the all-important part with the principle being to start the ball spinning as it is being projected forward.

For the off break, the top joint of the first finger should grip across the seam of the ball (the stitching) and this becomes the main spinning lever. The second finger, which should be well spaced away from the first, also grips across the seam with the thumb lying along the seam.

The grip for an off break. The two top fingers are well spaced and placed along the seam.

The spin is given by the wrist being cocked back and then snapped forward with the first finger dragging sharply downwards and the thumb flipping upwards. After the ball has been delivered, the hand cuts across the body with the palm pointing upwards.

For the leg break, the top joint of the thumb and first two fingers are spaced apart gripping across the seam. The third finger cups the ball and lies along the seam to produce the leg spin. The wrist is bent inwards and only snaps straight as the ball is delivered. The third and fourth fingers flick upwards and forwards while the thumb side of the hand snaps down. After delivery, the hand finishes with the palm upwards.

The off break is less dangerous than the leg break and needs variation of spin, length, width and pace to achieve much effect. An underpitched off break is of no value and any deviation of direction in straying to the legside will make it an easy ball to sweep or glide away.

Leg breaks should be pitched well up on or just outside leg stump compelling the batsman to come forward. By a very extreme turn of the wrist the googly is effected (a ball bowled with a leg-break action, but breaking from the off instead).

How to succeed with spin: try to get the batsman reaching forwards without getting to the pitch of the ball and so bowling him; lure him out in an attempt to achieve a full toss; encourage him to hit against the spin at a ball not quite up to him; send down a succession of leg breaks on leg stump, then try a top spin

The grip for a leg break. The third finger lies parallel to the seam with the top joints of the first two fingers directly upon the seam.

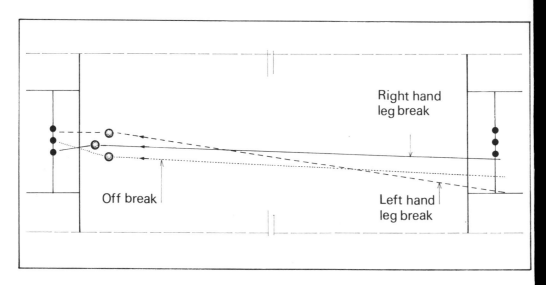

**Diagram 8**: The off break and leg break.

or googly pitching on off stump. The batsman may be fooled into thinking it is another off break.

### The Slow Left-Armer
Until now we have talked solely in terms of the right-hander both in batting and bowling and invited the left-handed player simply to reverse the process. But in slow bowling, the left-armer comes into an exclusive category.

For the leg break comes much more easily to the left-armer and can be a positively lethal delivery.

The ball is flighted from the offside to leg, then either breaks back from leg or straightens. The left-armer must create doubt about the length of delivery. He uses the same technique as the leg-breaker, but more flexibility of pace is possible.

He can also bowl the ball that continues its course from the off after it has pitched – that is, goes straight on with the arm and is achieved by using no wrist turn in the delivery.

Then there is the ball which pitches outside off stump and breaks in front from the off. This is known as the chinaman.

The slow left-armer should always bowl in such a way that the ball can only be hit into the offside field. He should crowd that side with fielders as the batsman will always court danger if he tries to play against the spin to leg.

### General Bowling Tips
In collaboration with his captain, the bowler must decide his placing of fielders. The usual field is for an inner ring of fielders and an outer ring for the hard-hit shots. Do not be afraid to 'crowd' an incoming batsman with one or two extra fielders brought up into close catching positions as he tentatively plays his first few balls. Also arrange some pre-determined signal to send a fielder into some position where you are hoping to lure a batsman

into hitting the ball for a possible catch.

Always be on the alert for the possible caught-and-bowled chance when completing the follow-through to your delivery. And get back sharply behind the stumps to receive the return throw from a fielder when a batsman goes for a run. A run-out may be the result of such quick-thinking. Never, however, stand in front of the stumps or halfway down the wicket when waiting for the return.

Particularly if you are a fast bowler, have no qualms about letting mid-off, mid-on or one of the close fielders stoop to pick up shots anywhere in your area as this is simply a sensible method of not unduly wasting energy. Another tip when you have been called on to start a bowling spell – bowl a few 'looseners' to your nearest fielder before starting your first over.

Never be afraid to ask for sawdust to be put down on your run-up and a towel to dry off the ball when bowling in wet conditions after rain. This avoids the possibility of losing control or even injury to yourself.

And again, if you are a fast or medium-pace bowler, keep shining the ball on your flannels (you can also use sweat from your forehead) so that it goes on swerving for as long as possible.

One final tip (for the sake of players and public alike): Try to bowl your overs fairly briskly in the interests of keeping the game on the move.

## The lbw law

All bowlers must be aware of the interpretation of the leg-before-wicket dismissal. The batsman is out if, with any part of his person except his hand, which is in a straight line between wicket and wicket, he intercept a ball which has not first touched his bat or hand and which, in the opinion of the umpire, shall have pitched on a straight line from the bowler's wicket to the striker's wicket, or shall have pitched on the offside of the striker's wicket, provided always that the ball would have hit the wicket.

All four of the following questions have to be answered in the affirmative if a batsman is to be adjudged lbw: Would the ball have hit the wicket? Did the ball pitch on a straight line between wicket and wicket (and this includes a ball intercepted at full pitch by the striker) or did it pitch on the offside of the striker's wicket? Was it part of the striker's person other than the hand which first intercepted the ball? Was that part of the striker's person in a straight line between wicket and wicket at the moment of impact irrespective of the height of the point of impact?

The following experimental law currently applies to lbw: Should the umpire be of the opinion that the striker has made no genuine attempt to play the ball with his bat, he shall, on appeal, give the striker out lbw if he is satisfied that the ball would have hit the stumps even though the ball pitched outside the off stump and even though any interception was also outside the off stump.

# Chapter Four
# Fielding

Although the diehards of cricket forcibly denounce the artificiality of the limited-overs game (i.e. Gillette Cup, Benson and Hedges Cup and the John Player League), because of such supposed blemishes as careless shots, shortened run-ups for bowlers and little encouragement for the spinner, even they are obliged to admit that the advent of this exciting brand of cricket has brought about an immense improvement in fielding standards at all levels of cricket.

The reckless pursuit of runs has sharpened up a side of the game which was somewhat overlooked in the past and even regarded as a chore by most of those who were not in close catching positions.

In the first-class game today few fielders are put in out-of-the-way places where they are unlikely to be engaged in much activity. In fact, however skilled may be a batsman or bowler, his fielding ability must be acceptable as well.

As in first-class games, so the standard in lower levels of cricket has improved out of all recognition as well and this has been nothing but beneficial to the youngster who, although perhaps not particularly proficient with bat or ball, is a real enthusiast and can still earn his place in a side by his alertness in the field.

**The Positions**
Fielders fall into two categories – the close catcher and the outfielder, and it should become quickly apparent which is the most suitable category for you.

Collecting and returning a ball at speed. The fielder gets both hands behind the ball and allows it to run into them. The right foot is turned at right angles both to form a barrier and turn the body sideways to the wicket for a fast return throw.

The close catcher needs a quick eye and good reactions; the outfielder must be a fleet runner, adept at holding high catches and equipped with a strong and accurate throw.

Close catchers comprise the slip fielders, gully, point, short leg, silly mid-on and silly mid-off.

The outfielder takes up his position in deep positions such as third man, long-leg, long-on and long-off. In rather more attacking positions come cover, square-leg, mid-wicket, mid-off and mid-on.

The most demanding fielding position (apart from wicketkeeping which will be dealt with in the next chapter), however, is in the slip area where sometimes three, or even four, players may be placed. Although not much physical exertion is required, the slip fielder needs the utmost mental concentration for he has only a split second in which to react after the ball leaves the edge of the bat. Success or failure in cutting off an edged snick or taking the sharpest of catches is as finely defined as that. This all means fine eyesight, razor-sharp reflexes and never any day-dreaming! The catch the fielder hopes for is one which flies off the edge of the bat at stomach-height as he crouches, hands cupped. All too often, however, the catch comes at bootstrap-height and requires a lunge or even a dive. The best way to sharpen up reflexes is to use a wooden contraption called a cradle. It consists of strips of wood in a sort of semi-circle from which a cricket ball comes out at all angles.

The other close catchers in front of the wicket must be on the alert for the ball that pops up off the bat and pad or is flicked a few inches off the ground into the legside. Their hands will not sting so much since, unlike the catch that flies off the edge to slip, the ball will not come at them with anything like the same speed.

Of the fielders further from the bat, the covers undoubtedly occupy the most crucial area. This is an important placing because most balls bowled pitch on or outside off stump and, in

consequence, most of the batsman's shots will be placed in the direction of the cover arc.

The cover fielder should be about 20 or 30 yards from the bat and be able to swoop easily on the ball, which could often be a full-blooded off-drive, pick up with either hand cleanly and return the ball smartly, swiftly and low over the stumps to the wicketkeeper. Cover will also face some fiercely-struck catches so he must be constantly on his toes.

Mid-off is a position most favoured by the captain of the side unless he is a specialist in some other placing. This is because there he is nearest to his bowler and thus able easily to direct field alterations or give advice to his bowler. He will be about 20–25 yards from the bat and, like cover, will have quite an amount of work to do from the offside shots. He will also need a strong pair of hands as the catches that come his way will be driven off the full face of the bat.

Third man may not be a position in which to pull off any spectacular catches, but it is strategically important since the cuts and edges that will inevitably elude the slips will all come his way. He will have to be quick on his feet and able to stoop and pick up on the run as he patrols a fairly wide area of the boundary. He will not be able to stop the batsmen taking a single, but he can stop them turning one run into two or even a boundary. He will, too, have to possess a good throwing arm.

Long-off and long-on will only be field placings when a batsman is in full command and hitting out. Like third man their job will be to stop singles being converted into twos, but they will also have the chance of lofted catches.

But what about that one member of the fielding side with neither the speed of thought or of foot? Where should he be 'hidden'? Mid-on is the most likely position. This is because batsmen tend not to play too many shots in this direction. It is far

Retrieving a slow ball. The fielder gets down to block the ball with his body and lets it run into his hands so avoiding misfields.

Ian Botham taking a catch in the outfield.

more common to off-drive than on-drive, just as anything played on the onside is usually placed in the extensive arc from mid-wicket to long leg.

## On the Alert

Whether in the deep or close in, the fielder must be ready to make the fastest possible move to any ball that comes his way.

For those fielding deep at cover, mid-off and mid-on, the main task is to stop ground shots and save runs and if they are already moving as the ball is bowled, they will be all the better equipped to do so. One can easily tell the trained fielder by noting whether he is walking in as the bowler runs in, rather like a stalking cat.

Close fielders, of course, crouch motionless, ready for a ball coming head-high or at their toes. They should also be on their toes, too, with weight evenly divided so that they can move either way.

## Throwing

For the strongly-built fielder, throwing in presents no problem; for those, however, who cannot propel the ball great distances the basic art of throwing can still be accomplished reasonably satisfactorily if a few basic tips are remembered.

Try to achieve a full toss throw straight into the wicketkeeper's gloves by aiming at a point a few inches above the stumps (a good keeper acknowledges such a return with the raising of his gloved hand after a sweep of his hands over the stumps).

If the thrower is not strong enough to achieve a full toss, he should try to propel a long-hop to the keeper's gloves. Any ball that arrives around the keeper's feet is a bad return, for he cannot quickly sweep off the bails in any run-out attempt.

The ball should never be returned from the deep field to the bowler's end, unless again a run-out chance is in the offing. The bowler is one of the team's assets and does not want to risk injury to his hands in trying to catch a hard full toss return or one

Taking a skied catch. While watching the ball at all times, move underneath it and hold your cupped hands at about chin height. As you take the catch relax your hands slightly to stop the ball bouncing out.

pitching awkwardly around his feet. He will even let the ball overrun the stumps if he fears a painful blow to his hands and this brings in the importance of backing up.

Whenever a fielder returns the ball, one or more fielders should get in line with the throw behind the wicketkeeper to avoid the danger of an overthrow and unnecessary extra runs. Overthrows are the sloppiest sight in a fielding side and cast question on discipline under the captain.

**Catching**

'Catches win matches' – the phrase explains the most vital part of fielding. The catch comes in two categories: the close catch taken near the bat and the lengthy judged catch.

For the slip fielder, it is important to know how far back from the wicket to stand and this is determined by judging just how fast the pitch is. The faster it is, the further back he will be to give himself that vital extra fraction of time to make his catch. The fingers of the hand are initially cupped and will be turned towards the ground and ready to yield under the impact. The harder the catch, the more the hands must yield or else there is the danger of the ball bouncing out again.

The judged catch is that in which the outfielder has the time to assess the flight of the ball. Too often a fielder runs in too soon and finds that the ball is going to sail over his head.

Having assessed the flight, the fielder should try and cover the ground needed before preparing to make the catch. A ball taken on the run may look spectacular, but there is the risk that it may bounce out of his hands because he is not correctly balanced.

The correct position to take the lofted catch is with cupped hands at chest-height, with knees bent and hands yielding.

Judged catching should be straightforward if these rules are followed, but it is always as well before a match for a group of players to get together and take it in turns with a bat to loft catches at their colleagues.

# Chapter Five
# Wicketkeeping

The most industrious member of a fielding side is the wicketkeeper for, unlike anyone else, he is actively involved with every ball of the innings, crouching behind the stumps prepared to take every ball bowled, alert for catches and stumpings, ready to run to the legside to stop snap singles, capable of taking cleanly everything thrown to him from the fielders and is also able to advise a bowler on some technical point from his perfect position of vision.

It is an exhausting job for the mentally alert and some measure of the strain may be found in the case of Derek Taylor, the Somerset wicketkeeper who demonstrates the various stances in the accompanying pictures. Two or three years ago, he was highly successfully converted from a No. 8 batsman into an opener whose ability to score runs as well as keep wicket so competently earned him selection for England Trial and MCC representative matches. But Derek, after a season and a half of opening the batting, asked to be returned down the order as he found the physical strain of a long day behind the stumps followed immediately by the need to go back out in front of the stumps was too exhausting. The story shows that any aspiring wicketkeeper will have to be prepared to work really hard at the job.

Standing right up to the wicket for medium and slow bowling. The wicketkeeper has bent completely down and has both hands together with palms up.

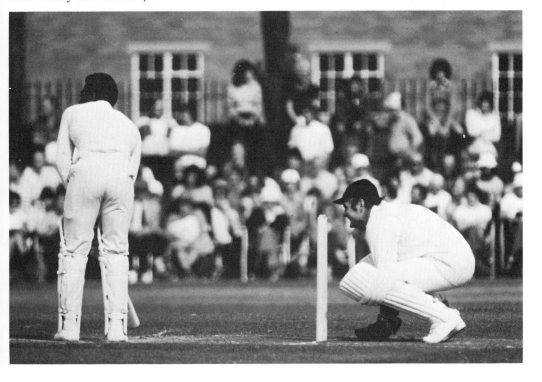

## Equipment

No wicketkeeper can hope to do himself justice unless his equipment – gloves and pads – are adequate. He should wear gloves that are large enough to allow at least one pair of inner (ordinary, thin) gloves which should fit the hands loosely. These 'inners' must also be big enough to take extra padding in the

Even after the stroke has been made the wicketkeeper should still remain alert and ready for a possible running out.

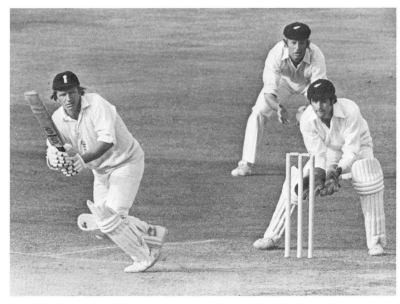

As the ball pitches the wicketkeeper, Derek Taylor, moves towards it and collects it with both hands.

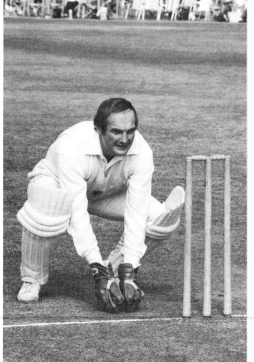

protection of the hands, but the amount of padding should not be such that the keeper is unable to get a good grip of the ball.

The outer gloves need plenty of protection or else they will become hard and slippery. Eucalyptus oil or saddler's soap will keep the leather in good condition and a little resin will provide the desired slightly sticky effect. But do not overdo this preparation or else the ball will become a bit sticky which will hardly please bowlers.

Pads should be sturdy, although these do not tend to be as floppy and outsize in comparison with batting pads as in former days. Remember, however, that pads are primarily for protection and a good wicketkeeper will not use his pads to stop the ball unless absolutely necessary.

## Standing Up

The wicketkeeper should always get as good a sight of the ball as possible, never allowing the batsman to impede his view. This is achieved by squatting on the offside of the wicket with the left toe in line with the off stump about 18 inches behind.

As the bowler begins his run-up, the keeper's hands should be on the ground with the palms upwards and arms between the knees with heels on the ground. As he prepares to receive the ball – the batsman having either played and missed or offered no shot – the weight is transferred from the heels to the toes as he moves from the squat position to the crouch to receive the ball.

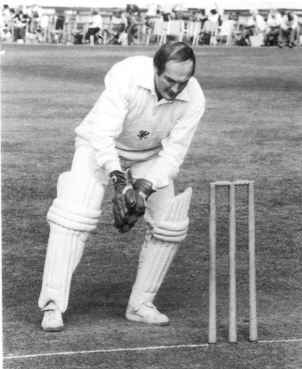

When there is a possibility of a running out the wicketkeeper should move up to and around the wicket to face the fielder. Here Asif Iqbal has made his run by grounding his bat even though he himself is outside the crease.

Remember to rise only after the ball has pitched. It is pointless to get up too early.

Every ball should be taken in both hands unless the delivery is so wide of the wicket that the keeper has to dive to legside or offside. Fingers should be pointed towards the ground with hands together and palms facing the bowler. The hands, too, should never be moved forward to take the ball as if to snatch it. Always allow it to come into the cupped hands in its own time and also allow the hands to yield a little upon impact.

The body should be close behind the hands, but if the ball deviates somewhat move only the right foot to deliveries wide of the off stump and vice versa to the leg. Although it is acceptable to move sideways, never take a step back in receiving the ball.

### Standing Back

In junior cricket, schoolboys sometimes think it is rather feeble and 'cissy' to stand well back to fast bowling. But this is totally wrong.

If the keeper stands too far up to the wicket in a spirit of bravado he may well suffer injury – let alone miss catches – and with the recognised keeper out of the action a fielding side is sorely handicapped.

The keeper is far more comfortable if he stands well back to fast bowling. Ideally he should be able to take the ball on the long hop,

A wicketkeeper taking an edged catch when standing back for fast bowling.

i.e. at comfortable catching height. Stumpings are obviously out of the question, but he is at the right distance to take those edged catches.

But the keeper standing back to the quick bowling must always hurry up to the stumps if the batsman strikes the ball so that he is smartly in position to take the ball over the bails when the fielder's return throw comes in. One questionable point when the keeper is standing back is whether he should dive across the first slip fielder when a batsman edges a ball in that direction. The problem is that he may well unsight the first slip and also miss the catch himself. Only the supremely confident keeper should take this sort of risk.

**Catching**

Once the wicketkeeper has mastered the art of taking everything cleanly in his two gloves, he should be capable of taking most catches that come his way, especially when standing up to the medium-pace and slow bowlers.

The ball that comes off the edge of the bat to the keeper standing up will not really deviate at all before it has landed in the gloves. Consequently the keeper does not need to move his hands at all when he hears the snick off the edge.

When standing back to the quick bowlers, he has a fraction more time before the ball lands in his gloves. Avoid the temptation to move the hands forward on hearing a snick. You are snatching for the ball and will probably put it down.

The keeper, too, should be the one fielder to appeal for a catch.

After collecting the ball from the fielder the wicketkeeper should sweep his hands over the stumps to acknowledge a good throw.

Yet often all the slips throw up their hands in noisy unison and, in theory, could panic the keeper into snatching too soon.

## Stumping and Running Out

When standing up, the keeper, on taking the ball, should sweep his gloves above the wicket. As mentioned earlier in the section on fielders' throwing, he does this to acknowledge a good return throw. He should do this also when the ball beats the bat because there could be a clear chance of a stumping. Keepers get fairly few real stumping chances, but they always bring satisfaction because they are the keeper's most spectacular contribution. A successful stumping requires split-second reflexes so one foot should always be near the stumps. Again, do not snatch at the ball and remember above all that the ball cannot be taken until it has passed the stumps.

Slow bowling provides the best opportunity for stumping as a batsman is lured forward and beaten by the spin. The keeper should always watch the bowler's hand at the point of delivery to see what sort of ball he intends to bowl. Often keepers and spin bowlers operate a secret signalling code to determine the next delivery.

Leg breaks tend to produce most stumping chances, whereas off breaks tend to be more difficult to make into a stumping.

Running out opportunities are simply a matter of standing behind the stumps, facing the fielder and gathering the ball cleanly before breaking the wicket with a sweep of the hand.

A successful stumping. Watching the delivery at all times, the wicketkeeper sways towards the wicket even before collecting the ball and hits the stumps in one flowing movement.

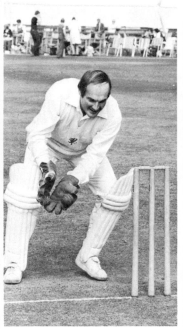

## Chapter Six
# Captaincy

It does not necessarily follow that the star member of a cricket team will be the captain. But the captain must be a natural leader, capable of handling people, of setting an example by enthusiasm and alertness in the field, even a psychologist inasmuch as he must be able to handle the varying temperaments of team members. He must also be a good reader of the game – able to exploit all the tactical options open to him.

### Selecting the Side
Possibly he will work with a selection committee, but basically the captain has the final say in naming his side. Ideally it is composed of five front-line batsmen, an allrounder adept with both bat and ball, the wicketkeeper and four main bowlers.

His batting line-up begins with an opening pair who will probably differ in technique. One will be the natural stroke player who will look for runs from the start of the innings; the other will adopt the 'sheet anchor' role, aiming to remain at the wicket for some time even if he is not scoring so freely as his partner. Ideally this means that the opening pair are together for some time, a reasonable scoring rate is being maintained and both are blunting the threat of the new ball attack for the stroke-makers to follow.

Batsmen three, four and five will all be looking to make useful scores; batsman six will probably be the allrounder with an attacking ability to 'get after' the bowling. Then comes the wicketkeeper (unless he is an exceptional batsman) and the specialist bowlers – the tailend 'rabbits' with few real pretensions to being batsmen.

In the field, the captain will want a bowling strength made up of the front-line assault of two opening fast bowlers with a couple of medium-pacers as his first-change bowlers. A slow bowler – ideally a left-arm leg-break specialist – will complete the attack.

### Bowling and Field Placing
Bowlers are a breed of players far more given to temperament than batsmen. Perhaps this is because of the great physical and mental strain imposed upon them, perhaps because a batsman who hits a century will enjoy more popular acclaim than the bowler who takes five, six or seven wickets in an innings.

For whatever reason, the captain handles his bowling attack with care and consideration.

Some bowlers can operate for long spells, others prefer short bursts. The captain must know all about his men and be able to spot when one of them is tiring and take him out of the attack for a breather.

Obviously, if the state of the wicket is to the bowler's liking and he is claiming victims, then his tail will be up and he will be spurred to bowl on for a longer spell than normal. But if the wicket is offering little encouragement to the bowling side, then the captain should constantly make bowling changes in an attempt to unsettle the batsmen by regularly confronting them with different types of attack.

In compliance with his bowler's wishes, the captain must always be ready to vary his field placings. If the bowler is being hit about the field, then the captain must try to plug the gaps. When a wicket falls he must call up extra close catchers to crowd the incoming batsman. If he knows his opponents well he should also attempt to exploit their weaknesses. At first-class level, cricketers have a most effective intelligence network so that they know the strengths and weaknesses of all their opponents on the county circuit. The system comes unstuck, however, when a young newcomer arrives on the scene. If really talented, he will often make a big initial impact and then find himself struggling for runs or wickets when his second season comes around. For, by then, his strengths and weaknesses will have been passed along the county grapevine and only the player of real character and quality will survive.

*Above left:* A heavily-armoured Mike Brearley, captain of the England team which won back the Ashes in 1977 and defended them successfully in Australia in 1978–79. Brearley's adoption of a helmet as protection against fast bowling caused a lot of controversy, but has been widely followed.

*Above:* Arnold Long, the Sussex captain, holding the Gillette Cup they won in 1978. One of the comparatively few wicketkeepers to captain a side, his experienced leadership played a crucial part in his team's success.

## Exploiting the Elements

The captain must have a sound knowledge of conditions peculiar to cricket such as the way in which the weather may affect a match. So, having won the toss, he must have a good look at the wicket before deciding whether to bat or field.

If the pitch is heavy and sodden, he should elect to bat first because there will be little or no pace in the pitch and the batsmen will have all the time in the world to play the ball.

If the weather, rather than the wicket, is heavy and humid, he should always field first provided he has the fast bowlers who can make the ball swing and swerve in these helpful conditions.

If hot sun has replaced recent rain, then the wicket will be sticky and spiteful and if he has good spinners to back up his pace attack they will have a field day.

But if the day is fine and the wicket hard, conditions should be perfect for batting and he will want first use of a pitch that will wear with use and offer some help to his bowlers later on.

All this assumes the captain has won the toss. But what if he loses it? He still has a decision to take should the other side have opted to bat first. When his team's turn comes to bat, the captain must decide whether the light or heavy roller should be used on the wicket before his side bats.

The light roller should be used when the wicket is dry, but in danger of breaking up. A soft wicket should be treated with the heavy roller because it will make a damp surface relatively mild in the early part of an innings, allowing his batsmen plenty of time to sight the ball.

**Batting and Declarations**
As with his bowling changes and field placings, a captain has authority over his batsmen. Ideally he should allow them to play in their natural styles unless a chase for victory or a struggle to draw takes preference.

No hard and fast rules apply to declarations, except that a captain should never leave his declaration so late that the opposition have not even a sporting chance of achieving their set target. The state of the wicket, the strength of the opposition batting – these factors must be borne in mind before setting a target that ideally gives both sides an equal chance of winning.

**The Ambassador**
Because cricket is still quaintly regarded as a gentleman's game (although that is something of a debating point in the 1970s) the captain should set an example both on and off the field. That means making sure his side is smartly turned out (pads and boots whitened, flannels pressed, etc.). It means quickly intervening in any onfield dispute and making sure his side do not dissent from a dubious umpiring decision too obviously. A captain in cricket, in fact, probably undertakes more overall responsibility than in any other sport. He must be a disciplinarian, he must be an ambassador and above all he must be a real sportsman.

Chapter Seven
# The Game's Structure

All cricket in the UK – from Test Match level to the schools and village game – comes under the umbrella of the Cricket Council.

Until 1966 and the formation of the Sports Council, the responsibility for the running of the game belonged to the MCC (the Marylebone Cricket Club), which had been formed in 1787 with one Thomas Lord providing his ground in Dorset Fields, St Marylebone and whose own name was to be immortalised by the game's headquarters – Lord's Cricket Ground.

When the Sports Council was introduced in 1966 it asked the MCC to set up an official body since it could not deal with what was after all a private club. Thus the Cricket Council which has three main departments – the Test and County Cricket Board (TCCB), the MCC itself and the National Cricket Association (NCA).

The TCCB is in charge of all Test Matches and first-class cricket in the country, all overseas tours, all the various one-day limited-over competitions, the County Championship and the Minor Counties Championship (the league for those counties without first-class status).

The headquarters of cricket – Lord's Cricket Ground.

The MCC, in conjunction with all overseas cricket-playing countries, is responsible for any changes in the laws and the NCA covers what the TCCB does not – cricket in schools, the services, the women's game and at club level.

**Test Cricket**

The above organisations deal with the domestic game, while on a world-wide scale the sport comes under the auspices of the International Cricket Conference (ICC) which was founded in 1909.

Test Matches are played between the full member-countries which are Australia, England, India, New Zealand, Pakistan and the West Indies (when South Africa withdrew from the British Commonwealth she ceased to be a full member, but remains eligible for re-admission, while the most recent country to seek, as yet unsuccessfully, full status is Sri Lanka – formerly Ceylon – which currently plays 'unofficial' Tests as part of a proving process).

Although, somewhat incredibly, the first known international cricket match took place in the last century between such improbable opponents as Canada and the United States of America, the first official Test Match took place at Melbourne in 1877 between Australia and England.

Tests are played in series (normally of five matches), one country touring another, the rota for such tours being arranged by the ICC. Tests are usually of five days' duration and the laws are more or less the same as in English first-class cricket, although

Slip fielders Keith Stackpole and Ian Chappell fail to stop a shot from Barry Wood in this Test Match between England and Australia.

The scoreboard at Trent Bridge showing the complexity of the information that can be transmitted to the spectator. Among other things, the scoreboard shows the current total, the batsman's scores, the bowling figures and the scores at which each wicket fell.

there are some slight differences such as interpretation of the lbw law, while in Australia and New Zealand, for instance, the bowler's over consists of eight deliveries instead of the six in the English game.

The most famous Test series is that played between England and Australia and is known as the fight for the Ashes.

Two circumstances brought about the origin of the Ashes. In 1882 Australia beat England at The Oval and an obituary appeared on 30 August 1882 in the London *Sporting Times*: 'In affectionate remembrance of English Cricket which died at The Oval 29 August 1882, deeply lamented by a large circle of sorrowing friends and acquaintances RIP. N.B: the body will be cremated and the Ashes taken to Australia'!

A year later an England team in Australia won a Test series and some ladies burnt a bail after the final Test, placed its ashes in a small urn and presented it to the England captain, the Hon.

One of the most beautiful grounds in England – Worcestershire Cricket Ground with the 12th-century cathedral dominating the horizon.

Ivo Bligh. These Ashes were later given to the MCC and are kept permanently at Lord's.

## The County Championship

With the advent of sponsorship, this tournament is now known as the Schweppes Championship, but it has been in existence since 1864 when Surrey became the first champions.

Seventeen counties compete: Derbyshire, Essex, Glamorgan, Gloucestershire, Hampshire, Kent, Lancashire, Leicestershire, Middlesex, Northamptonshire, Nottinghamshire, Somerset, Surrey, Sussex, Warwickshire, Worcestershire and Yorkshire.

Over the years the rules have regularly been revised and with the introduction of the one-day limited-overs game in the 1960s, the Championship has been much reduced in content to allow time to be put aside for the various other competitions.

Today each county plays 22 three-day matches – one against each of the others and, unsatisfactorily, a return fixture against only six of them.

Twelve points are awarded for a win. In addition there is a maximum of eight bonus points for batting and bowling, in the first innings only. A batting point is gained when the total reaches 150, 200, 250 and 300; a bowling point is awarded when three, five, seven and nine wickets are down. Also in the first innings, the side batting first is allocated only 100 overs and if dismissed inside this amount, the surplus overs are available to the side batting second. This first innings limit on overs is a fairly recent innovation, but has drastically reduced the number of rather meaningless drawn matches, which always used to be the bane of the competition.

## Limited-Overs Cricket

Although the limited-overs game of 'instant' cricket has captured a huge public of enthusiasts and spread right through the game to the most junior level, students of cricket technique must be warned that they will see much that does not belong in the text book as players abandon all pretence to orthodoxy in the hectic chase for success. But, be that as it may, the limited-overs game is great fun and has most definitely established its place of importance in the way cricket is played. Indeed, cricket was dying on its feet for lack of interest, particularly among young people, before the Gillette Cup changed all that when launched in 1963.

It is a knockout competition – cricket's FA Cup – between the 17 first-class counties and the five leading sides in the previous season's Minor Counties Championship. Matches are of 60 overs per side – each bowler being limited to an allocation of 12 overs – the Cup Final being played on the first Saturday in September at Lord's . . . always a major event in the cricket calendar and it attracts a capacity crowd.

The Benson and Hedges Cup is the younger knockout competition, having been launched in 1972. This is of 55 overs a side (bowlers 11 overs each). It differs from the Gillette in that the 17 counties plus three sides drawn from the Minor Counties and combined Oxford and Cambridge Universities are divided into four zones and play each other on a league basis. The top two in each section go forward to the quarter-finals and the competition continues on a knockout basis with the final at Lord's in July.

The third of the first-class limited-overs competitions is the John Player Sunday League in which the 17 first-class counties play each other once. Matches are limited to 40 overs a side (play

A batsman hitting out in a Gillette Cup match between Lancashire and Kent.

Cricket is played on village greens the length and breadth of the country — much of it in as idyllic a setting as Harstbourne Priors, Hampshire.

does not start until 2 pm) with the bowlers limited not only to eight overs each but also with their run-ups reduced to 15 yards. This, then, is the most artificial of the limited-overs competitions, but it is enormously popular with the public.

From these first-class competitions have evolved tournaments of a similar nature in all classes of cricket, notably the Village Knockout competition, which attracts an annual entry of approaching 1000 British villages.

Finally, to emphasise the impact of the limited-overs game, it has even become international. All the member countries of the International Cricket Conference now arrange a series of one-day matches when one country is touring another.

W. G. Grace would turn in his grave to see Lord's, on the first Saturday in September, transformed into a packed arena of banner-waving, cheering, singing stronghold of supporters, but this brand of cricket has become the game's lifeblood.

**The Packer Affair**

Cricket was turned upside down in 1977 by an Australian television tycoon called Kerry Packer who signed up most of the world's greatest players in stealth and staged a series of show matches – both on Test lines and at limited-overs level – in Australia. By great good fortune for the official administrators of cricket, his coup was considerably harmed by an absorbing official Test series between Australia and India which had the Australian public totally engrossed.

Clearly, collaboration between the game's governors and Packer is necessary. The Australian has the immense advantage of being able to argue convincingly that, by his intervention, the Establishment has had to adjust its previously niggardly attitude towards the earnings of cricketers. The game now provides a worthwhile income for the humblest of players.

# Glossary

Cricket is full of curiosities, not least in its dialogue. These are some of the words and expressions which constantly crop up, especially in television commentaries.

**Against the Clock** When a batting side is set a victory target requiring them to score at a faster rate than a run a minute.
**Allrounder** A player competent at both batting and bowling.
**Appeal against the Light** When visibility is too poor, the batsmen are given the invitation to come off the field until the light improves.
**At Stumps** At the close of play, when the stumps are removed.
**Awarded a Cap** When a player has proved his ability, it is customary to award him the official club cap.
**Backing Up** Starting down the pitch by the non-striking batsman as the ball is bowled in case his colleague can get a run.
**Bails** The two objects that lodge on top of the stumps which must be dislodged to effect a dismissal.
**Bowling Spell** The consecutive overs bowled by one player.
**Carrying One's Bat** An opening batsman who stays unbeaten while the rest of his side are dismissed.
**Clean Bowled** When a bowler strikes middle stump. *Also called* bowled neck and crop.
**Crease** The line drawn in front of the stumps marking the boundary of the area inside which the batsman cannot be stumped.
**Dead Ball** When the ball is in the wicketkeeper's gloves or fielder's hands, it marks the end of the action on a delivery by the bowler.
**Declaration** The voluntary close of its innings by the batting side even though all ten wickets have not been lost.
**Dolly Catch** A simple catch.
**Duck** Nought scored by a dismissed batsman.
**Extras** Runs scored but not by the batsmen. They are byes (runs taken when the keeper fails to stop a bowling delivery), leg byes (runs taken when the batsman plays a stroke and misses, but the ball rebounds off his pads), no balls (when a bowler oversteps his mark, the umpire calls 'no ball' and the batsman has a free shot. He can only be dismissed if he is run out.), wides (when the umpire deems a delivery too wide for the batsman to be able to reach the ball and one run is awarded).
**Following On** In a two-innings-a-side match, if one side trails by 150 runs after the first innings, they can be asked to begin immediately their second innings. In Test Matches, the margin of deficit has to be 200 or more.
**Gardening** When the batsman, between deliveries, walks down the wicket and prods the pitch with his bat because he thinks he has found a flaw on the surface.
**Gluepot** A wet pitch sweating under a hot sun.
**Grassing the Ball** Dropping a catch.
**Groping** Playing and missing the ball by the batsman.
**Hat-trick** Three wickets taken off successive balls by the same bowler.
**Having a Dip** Attempting a big hit.
**Holing Out** Hitting the ball high into the air to give an easy catch.
**Howzat** Literally, 'how was that?' – the appeal made by bowler or wicketkeeper for a catch, lbw, run out or stumping.
**King Pair** Being dismissed first ball in both first and second innings. *See* pair.
**Legside** The area behind the left-hand side of a batsman (the reverse for left-handed batsmen).
**Loosener** The first ball delivered by a new bowler in which he is more concerned with loosening up his muscles than striving for a wicket.
**Maiden** An over in which no runs are scored off the bat. A wicket maiden is achieved when, besides conceding no runs, the bowler also takes a wicket.
**Maiden Century** The first 100 scored in a batsman's career.
**Making One's Ground** Reaching the crease by a batsman after a run.
**Meaty Shot** A forceful shot off the middle of the bat.
**Nervous Nineties** So called because batsmen become ultra-cautious as they approach scoring 100.
**Nightwatchman** An unrecognised batsman who usually goes in at the tailend of the innings, but is promoted just before the close of play if a wicket has fallen and the captain does not wish to risk a recognised batsman for a few overs.
**Nudging** A shot that is pushed, rather than hit.
**Offside** The area of the field to the batsman's right (again the reverse if left-handed).
**Onside** The area in front of the batsman's left-hand side (the right side for left-handers).
**Over** Six consecutive deliveries by a bowler.
**Overthrow** A fielder's return which eludes the keeper so that the batsmen are able to take an extra run.
**Padding Up** Offering no stroke by a batsman who allows the ball to hit his pads (no leg bye allowed).
**Pair** A score of nought in successive innings of a match. *See* king pair.
**Rabbit** An unrecognised batsman.
**Ropes, Fence** The boundary perimeter.
**Run Out** A dismissal occurring when a fielder's return is too quick for a batsman who is stranded outside his crease when the keeper breaks the wicket.
**Safe Pair of Hands** A respected catcher.
**Sheet Anchor** A batsman who keeps his wicket intact while his colleagues are getting out.
**Sightscreen** The white backdrop at either end of the ground in line with the wickets to give the batsman a good sight of the ball.
**Six** A ball struck full toss over the boundary earns six runs. A four is scored when a shot reaches the boundary, but has at some stage touched the ground on its way.

**Square** The central area on a ground where pitches are prepared.
**Stand** A partnership between two batsmen.
**Stonewalling** Blocking each ball rather than intending to score runs.
**Stumps** The three sticks of wood at either end of the pitch which the bowler wants to hit and the batsman must defend.
**Tailender** One of the last batsmen; one unlikely to get many runs.
**Taking Guard** An incoming batsman asks the umpire to direct his bat in line with middle and leg stump, or middle stump.
**Taking One's Sweater** The end of a bowler's spell when he retrieves the sweater he has deposited with the umpire.

**Ton, Century** A score of 100 by a batsman.
**Twelfth Man** The reserve member of a team who fields as substitute if one of the team has to retire. He cannot, however, bat or bowl.
**Umpires** The two referees – one stands at the bowler's end and one at square leg (to adjudge stumpings and run outs).
**Using a Runner** When a batsman is handicapped by injury, but fit enough to bat, he is allowed to have a team-mate do the running for him. The runner stands in line with the wicket at square leg.
**Walking** The action of a sporting batsman who, knowing he has snicked a catch, immediately starts walking out before waiting to see the umpire confirm his dismissal.

## Acknowledgments

We should like to thank the following cricketers for their assistance: David Gurr, one of the unfortunately few genuine quick bowlers to emerge in England in the past few years; Philip Slocombe, technically one of the most talented young batsmen in England; Derek Taylor, one of the country's most consistent wicketkeepers who has been unfortunate not to progress further from Test trial matches.

The photographs in this book are by Tony Duffy/All Sport with the exception of the following: Central Press, London 32 above left, above, 56, 58; Patrick Eagar, London 15 bottom, 44 top, 46, 51 above left, above 53, 55; Sport and General, London 29; Syndication International, London 54, 57. Diagrams are by Chris Ake.

# Index

allrounder  8, 50
Ashes  55

back stroke  12, 13
batting stance  10
beamer  31
Benson and Hedges Cup  38, 57
bouncer  17, 18, 31

calling  23, 24
catching  42, 48, 49
concentration  11
county cricket  56
cowshot  20
cradle  39
cricket bat dimensions  9
Cricket Council  53
cross-batted strokes  16, 17, 19, 20
cut  16, 17

danger deliveries  21
declaring  52
delivery  26, 27, 28
drive  13, 14

fast bowling  21, 22, 29, 30, 31
field placings  38, 39, 40, 41, 50, 51
follow-through  29, 30
forward stroke  11, 12
full toss  25, 41

Gillette Cup  18, 38, 57
googly  35, 36
grip  10

half-volley  25
hook  17, 18, 19, 31

inswinger  30
International Cricket Council (ICC)  53, 58

John Player Sunday League  38, 57

leg before wicket (lbw)  37
leg break  34, 35, 36, 49
leg push  20
length and line  28
limited-overs cricket  23, 57, 58
long hop  25, 41
Lord's Cricket Ground  53

Marylebone Cricket Club (MCC)  53
medium bowling  32, 33
Minor Counties Championship  57

National Cricket Association (NCA)  53

off break  33, 34, 35, 36
outswinger  31

Packer, Kerry  58
pull  18, 19

Richards, Viv  18
running out  49
run-up  26, 27, 28, 29

Schweppes Championship  56
scoring leg  19, 20
selecting a side  50
slow bowling  22, 23, 49
spin bowling  33, 34
Sports Council  53
stumping  49
sweep  20

Taylor, Derek  43
Test and County Cricket Board (TCCB)  53
Test Cricket  54, 55
throwing  41, 42

weather conditions  51, 52
wicketkeeping equipment  44, 45
World Cup  8
wrist action  11 (batting)  28, 29 (bowling)

yorker  21, 22, 30